By Gloria Cruz

Illustrations by Clarice Elliott

Ready-to-Read

SIMON SPOTLIGHT

An imprint of Simon & Schuster Children's Publishing Division • New York   Amsterdam/Antwerp   London   Toronto   Sydney/Melbourne   New Delhi • 1230 Avenue of the Americas, New York, New York 10020 • For more than 100 years, Simon & Schuster has championed authors and the stories they create. By respecting the copyright of an author's intellectual property, you enable Simon & Schuster and the author to continue publishing exceptional books for years to come. We thank you for supporting the author's copyright by purchasing an authorized edition of this book. No amount of this book may be reproduced or stored in any format, nor may it be uploaded to any website, database, large language model, or other repository, retrieval, or artificial intelligence system without express permission. All rights reserved. Inquiries may be directed to Simon & Schuster, 1230 Avenue of the Americas, New York, NY 10020 or permissions@simonandschuster.com. • This Simon Spotlight edition June 2026 • Text © 2026 by Simon & Schuster, LLC • Illustrations © 2026 by Clarice Elliott • All rights reserved, including the right of reproduction in whole or in part in any form. SIMON SPOTLIGHT, READY-TO-READ, and colophon are registered trademarks of Simon & Schuster, LLC. For information about special discounts for bulk purchases, please contact Simon & Schuster Special Sales at 1-866-506-1949 or business@simonandschuster.com. Simon & Schuster strongly believes in freedom of expression and stands against censorship in all its forms. For more information, visit BooksBelong.com. The Simon & Schuster Speakers Bureau can bring authors to your live event. For more information or to book an event contact the Simon & Schuster Speakers Bureau at 1-866-248-3049 or visit our website at www.simonspeakers.com. Manufactured in the United States of America 0326 LAK • 2 4 6 8 10 9 7 5 3 1 • CIP data for this book is available from the Library of Congress. ISBN 9798347102006 (hc) • ISBN 9798347101993 (pbk) • ISBN 9798347102013 (ebook)

Glossary

ancestors: the people that someone descends from, usually more remote than a grandparent

charity: generosity and helpfulness toward those in need

cultures: groups with shared characteristics, such as beliefs, practices, and values

diyas: small oil lamps, usually made of clay

fasting: not eating some or all kinds of food or drink

heritage: qualities such as culture and tradition that are passed down from previous generations

joss paper: paper that symbolizes money and is burned as an offering

kinara: a branched candleholder with seven candlesticks used in celebrating Kwanzaa

lunar calendar: a calendar basing each month on a full cycle of the moon's phases

mosques: buildings used for worship in the Islamic faith

pi: an important number used in math and science, having an approximate value of 3.14

principles: rules or ideas for how to behave

Shawwal crescent moon: the sliver of the moon that is visible after the new moon at the end of Ramadan

Note to readers: Some of these words may have more than one definition. The definitions above match how these words are used in this book.

Contents

Note to readers: Many regions and cultures have special holidays. Here are just some of the occasions celebrated around the world.

Chapter 1:
Seasons

Around the world people come together to celebrate holidays and special occasions.

There are many important days
throughout the year that
are celebrated in different
cultures (say: KUHL-churz)
and communities.
Let's learn about
some of these holidays.

Lunar New Year is a cultural holiday celebrated in many countries in Asia and in Asian communities around the world. This festival celebrates the beginning of spring and the arrival of the new year.

Lunar New Year begins on the first
new moon of the **lunar calendar**
and ends on the first full moon.
People celebrate this holiday
with special meals, family
gatherings, and festive activities.

The Hungry Ghost Festival
is another seasonal holiday
celebrated in many Asian cultures
across the globe. It takes place
during the seventh month
of the lunar calendar, which is
in the summer.

During this holiday people honor their **ancestors** (say: AN-seh-sturz) and help calm wandering spirits that roam the earth. Families burn incense and **joss paper**, offer food, and light lanterns.

Many cultures celebrate the new year at different times. Rosh Hashanah (say: RAASH huh-SHAH-nuh) is a celebration of the Jewish New Year. This two-day holiday occurs on the first day of the seventh month of the Jewish calendar, which usually falls in autumn.

During Rosh Hashanah the shofar (say: SHOW-fahr), which is a trumpet made from a ram's horn, is blown many times each day. When people hear the shofar, they take time to think about their actions and focus on a fresh start in the new year.

Many people around the world enjoy Christmas.
This holiday marks the birth of Jesus Christ on December 25, but many cultures celebrate the spirit of Christmas in different ways throughout the month.

Some ways people celebrate Christmas include decorating fir (say: fur) trees, gifting presents, singing carols, hanging decorative lights, and enjoying delicious meals.

Chapter 2: Celebrate at Night

Some holidays are celebrated for a day. Others are celebrated over weeks.

And some holidays can be celebrated at night! Let's shine a light on some of these special celebrations.

Kwanzaa (say: KWAHN-zuh) is an African-American holiday that is celebrated over seven days from December 26 to January 1. This special occasion honors African-American culture, **heritage** (say: HEHR-uh-tij), and traditions.

Friends and families gather to
honor ancestors, give gifts,
share feasts, and celebrate bonds.
At the end of each night, people
light a **kinara** (say: kee-NAH-ruh)
candle that represents one of the
seven **principles**
(say: PRIN-suh-pulz) of Kwanzaa.

Diwali is the most important
holiday in Hinduism and is also
known as the Festival of Lights.
This five-day festival celebrates
the victory of light over darkness.

Some important traditions during Diwali include decorating homes, gathering with family, lighting **diyas** (say: DEE-yuhz), enjoying meals, exchanging gifts, and giving thanks.

Eid al-Fitr (say: EED-uhl-FIH-ter) is a significant Islamic holiday that marks the end of Ramadan (say: RAH-muh-dahn), which is a holy month of **fasting**, prayer, community, and **charity**. Eid al-Fitr begins at sunset after the **Shawwal** (say: SHAH-wahl) **crescent moon** has been spotted.

During Eid al-Fitr, people pray in **mosques** (say: MAWSKS), visit friends and family, give gifts, and gather for feasts.

There are many ways to celebrate
the new year. Some cultures follow
different calendars that determine
on which day the new year begins.
But in many places around the world,
new year celebrations begin on
the evening of December 31.

When the clock strikes midnight, people across the globe celebrate the new year. In Spain eating twelve grapes brings good luck. In Denmark people leap into the new year by jumping off chairs. Around the world people watch fireworks shows to celebrate.

Chapter 3:
Every Occasion

There are many important celebrations throughout the year. But some special occasions are celebrated just because they are fun!

On March 14, many people eat pie to celebrate Pi Day—a day that represents the first three digits of **pi** (π), 3.14.

Holidays bring people together,
and everyone around the world
can gather to celebrate
Earth Day on April 22.

On Earth Day people show their appreciation for Earth by planting trees, picking up litter, enjoying nature, saving water and energy, and more. This special day celebrates the beautiful planet we live on.

World Kindness Day on November 13 is another day when everyone around the world can gather to celebrate.

This special day is dedicated
to encouraging kindness, positivity,
and community. On this day
everyone comes together
to create a kinder world.

There are many significant holidays throughout the year. These important occasions celebrate culture and community around the world.

When people come
together to celebrate,
every day is a special day!

Celebrate Your Holiday!

Every day is a great day to celebrate! Now that you have learned about different holidays around the world, let's create and celebrate your own special day!

Here are a few questions to help you think of your holiday:

- When is your special occasion? Will it be celebrated for a week or for one day? How many days is it celebrated for?

- What will your holiday celebrate? Eating doughnuts? Doing opposite activities? Playing tag all day?

- How will you decorate for this holiday? With candles or confetti? Or with flowers and lights?

- What kind of food will you eat on this day? Yellow-colored food only? Or different potato dishes?

- Will you play games or give presents on your holiday?

Now let's invite your friends and family and have a celebration!